Smoothies
& Summer Drinks

pil

Publications International, Ltd.

Favorite Brand Name Recipes at www.fbnr.com

ISBN-13: 978-1-4127-2902-4
ISBN-10: 1-4127-2902-5

Manufactured in China.

87654321

pil
Publications
International, Ltd.

contents

14

72

86

frosty smoothies

COOL, CREAMY, SATISFYING TREATS

triple berry blast

. . . .

MAKES 2 (10-OUNCE) SERVINGS

1   cup frozen triple berry mix
1   cup soy milk*
½   cup sliced banana
2   teaspoons honey

Place all ingredients in blender. Blend on HIGH until smooth, thick and well combined, about 30 seconds. Serve immediately.

***Do not use vanilla-flavored soy milk because it will make the smoothie too sweet.**

Note: Soy milk is a ready-to-serve beverage often found in the refrigerated foods section near the yogurt or organic foods. It is made from soy beans and offers consumers the nutritional benefits of soy isoflavones, a class of antioxidants which some supporters believe may relieve some of the symptoms of menopause.

Sugar-Dipped Glasses: For a festive look and taste, add sugar to the rim of your glasses. Wet the rim with water, juice or by running a lime or lemon along the rim. Then, dip the glass in decorative sugar of your choice.

mandarin orange smoothie

MAKES 2¼ CUPS OR 3 (6-OUNCE) SERVINGS

1   can (11 ounces) mandarin orange sections, drained
1   cup orange sherbet
1   container (6 ounces) orange crème low-fat yogurt
½   cup orange-tangerine juice or orange juice, chilled

In a blender container combine orange sections, orange sherbet, yogurt and orange-tangerine juice. Cover and blend until nearly smooth. Serve in glasses.

berry blue smoothie

MAKES 4 SERVINGS (ABOUT 5 CUPS)

2   cups fresh or slightly thawed frozen blueberries
1   container (8 ounces) low-fat vanilla yogurt
1   cup milk
1   can (6 ounces) unsweetened pineapple juice
3   tablespoons honey
1½ cups ice cubes (about 16 cubes)

In an electric blender container place blueberries, yogurt, milk, pineapple juice and honey; blend until smooth. Add ice cubes, a few at a time, blend until finely crushed. Serve immediately.

Favorite recipe from **US Highbush Blueberry Council**

mandarin orange smoothie

banana split shakes

1   small (6-inch) ripe banana
¼   cup skim milk
5   maraschino cherries, drained
1   tablespoon light chocolate syrup
⅛   teaspoon coconut extract
4   cups chocolate low-fat frozen yogurt

1. Combine banana, milk, cherries, chocolate syrup and coconut extract in blender. Cover; blend on HIGH speed until smooth.

2. Add frozen yogurt 1 cup at a time. Cover and pulse on HIGH speed after each addition until smooth and thick. Pour into 4 glasses. Garnish with additional maraschino cherries, if desired.

Tip: For a low-fat shake, chop 3 large, peeled bananas. Place in resealable plastic bag and freeze until solid. (This is a great use for over-ripe bananas.) Blend with milk, cherries, chocolate syrup and coconut extract. It will not be as thick and frosty, but will be lower in calories and fat.

honeydew melon shake

1   cup honeydew melon chunks, chilled
½   cup vanilla low-fat yogurt
2   teaspoons sugar

Combine all ingredients in blender or food processor. Blend thoroughly. Pour and serve.

Variation: For strawberry melon flavor, blend in 1 cup frozen strawberries and add another teaspoon sugar.

Favorite recipe from **The Sugar Association, Inc.**

banana split shakes

kiwi pineapple cream

1   cup frozen pineapple chunks

1   container (6 ounces) Key lime yogurt

1   kiwi, peeled and sliced

½   cup canned unsweetened coconut milk

1   tablespoon honey

Place all ingredients in blender. Cover; process 15 to 30 seconds until smooth, using on/off pulsing action to break up chunks. Divide between 2 glasses and serve.

Kiwi Chai Smoothie: Add ¼ teaspoon vanilla, ⅛ teaspoon cardamom, ⅛ teaspoon ground cinnamon, ⅛ teaspoon ground ginger and a pinch of cloves to the mixture before blending.

Mango Smoothie

½ cup low-fat plain yogurt

1 ripe mango, peeled, seeded and diced

¼ cup orange-pineapple juice

1 teaspoon honey

2 ice cubes

Fresh mint leaves for garnish

Place all ingredients except mint leaves in blender container. Cover; blend until smooth. (Add milk if thinner consistency is desired.) Garnish, if desired.

Raspberry-Lemon Smoothie

MAKES ABOUT 1 ½ CUPS

1 cup frozen raspberries

1 carton (8 ounces) lemon-flavored yogurt

½ cup milk

1 teaspoon vanilla

Place all ingredients in blender. Cover; blend until smooth.

banana-coconut "cream pie" smoothie

3	medium-size ripe bananas
1½	cups coconut milk, chilled (do not use coconut cream)
1½	cups pineapple juice, chilled
½	teaspoon vanilla
2	tablespoons sugar
⅛	teaspoon ground nutmeg
3	ice cubes
	Toasted shredded sweetened coconut (optional)

1. Peel bananas and break into chunks. Place in blender container. Add coconut milk, pineapple juice, vanilla, sugar, nutmeg and ice cubes.

2. Blend on HIGH until mixture is frothy and ice cubes are finely ground, about 30 seconds to 1 minute. Pour into 4 glasses. Sprinkle on a little toasted coconut as a garnish.

Note: If desired, combine the ingredients in a large pitcher and purée using an immersion blender.

tropical mango frosty

1½	cups diced mango (2 mangoes)
½	cup orange juice
1	cup banana yogurt
½	cup ice cubes (about 4)

Place all ingredients in blender. Blend on HIGH until smooth and frothy, about 30 seconds.

banana-coconut
"cream pie"
smoothie

carrot cake smoothie

4   jars (4 ounces each) strained baby carrots

¼   cup sugar

½   teaspoon ground cinnamon

⅛   teaspoon ground ginger

    Dash ground nutmeg

    Dash salt

1   cup vanilla low-fat frozen yogurt

½   cup reduced-fat (2%) milk

2   ice cubes

4   long carrot sticks, optional

1. Combine baby carrots, sugar, cinnamon, ginger, nutmeg, salt, frozen yogurt, milk and ice cubes in blender container.

2. Blend on HIGH until mixture is frothy and ice cubes are finely ground, about 30 seconds to 1 minute. Pour into 4 glasses. Garnish each with 1 carrot stick for stirring. Serve immediately.

creamy fruit freeze

MAKES 4 SERVINGS

1   package (1 pound) frozen mixed fruit or peach slices, partially thawed

1   cup plain fat-free yogurt

½   cup orange juice

2   teaspoons grated fresh ginger

6   packets sugar substitute

1   teaspoon vanilla

Place all ingredients in blender and blend until smooth, scraping sides frequently. Serve immediately.

carrot cake smoothie

horchata shake

- 1 cup well-cooked rice (see note)
- 1 cup vanilla frozen rice milk ice cream substitute or 1 cup vanilla ice cream
- 2 cups rice milk or low-fat (1%) milk
- ¼ cup sugar
- ½ teaspoon cinnamon
- ½ teaspoon vanilla
- ¼ teaspoon salt
- 4 ice cubes

1. Combine rice, rice milk ice cream substitute, rice milk, sugar, cinnamon, vanilla, salt and ice cubes in blender container.

2. Blend on HIGH until mixture is frothy and ice cubes are finely ground, about 30 seconds to 1 minute.

3. Place a strainer over a pitcher. Pour the horchata through the strainer. Discard the puréed rice in the strainer. Serve immediately or chill for several hours. Stir well before pouring.

Note: Rice should be soft enough to mash with a fork.

raspberry smoothies

- 1½ cups fresh or frozen raspberries
- 1 cup plain sugar-free fat-free yogurt
- 1 cup crushed ice
- 1 tablespoon honey
- 2 packets sugar substitute or equivalent of 4 teaspoons sugar

Place all ingredients in food processor or blender; process until smooth. Serve immediately.

horchata shake

honeydew ginger smoothie

MAKES 2 (12-OUNCE) SERVINGS

1½	cups cubed honeydew melon
½	cup vanilla yogurt
¼	teaspoon grated ginger
½	cup sliced banana
½	cup ice cubes (about 4)

Place all ingredients in blender. Blend on HIGH until smooth, thick and well combined, about 30 seconds. Serve immediately.

strawberry & banana frostea

MAKES 5 (8-OUNCE) SERVINGS

1	cup boiling water
3	LIPTON® "Brisk" Cup Size Tea Bags or 1 Family Size Round Tea Bag
1	pint strawberries, hulled
1	banana, cut into chunks
¼	cup honey
3	cups ice cubes (about 18 to 24)

In teapot, pour boiling water over Lipton "Brisk" Cup Size Tea Bags; cover and brew 5 minutes. Remove Tea Bags; cool slightly.

In blender, process tea, strawberries, banana and honey. Add ice cubes, one at a time, and process until frosty. Serve immediately.

honeydew ginger smoothie

vermont maple smoothie

3   containers (½ cup each) unsweetened applesauce or
      1½ cups unsweetened applesauce

3   tablespoons maple syrup

½   teaspoon ground cinnamon

1   cup vanilla low-fat frozen yogurt

1   cup reduced-fat (2%) milk

2   ice cubes

    Ground nutmeg

1. Combine applesauce, maple syrup, cinnamon, frozen yogurt, milk and ice cubes in blender container. Blend on HIGH until mixture is frothy and ice cubes are finely ground, about 30 seconds to 1 minute.

2. Pour into 4 glasses. Top each with a light dusting of nutmeg.

Note: If desired, this can be made several hours in advance and chilled. Mix well before serving. The smoothie will not be as frothy.

piña colada cooler

MAKES 2 (12-OUNCE) SERVINGS

1¼   cups frozen diced pineapple*

¾   cup coconut sorbet

1   cup milk

Place all ingredients in blender. Blend on HIGH until smooth, thick and well combined, about 45 seconds.

Many supermarkets stock frozen diced pineapple in the frozen foods aisle with the other frozen fruits. To substitute fresh pineapple, peel and cut pineapple into ¼-inch dice. Arrange in a single layer in a resealable food storage bag and store in the freezer until frozen. Measure 1¼ cups of frozen diced pineapple and continue as above.

vermont maple smoothie

red raspberry smoothie

⅔ cup frozen red raspberries, partially thawed*

½ cup milk

½ cup vanilla frozen yogurt

¼ teaspoon vanilla

Whole red raspberries (optional)

To partially thaw raspberries, place them in a small bowl and microwave on LOW for 1 minute.

1. Place raspberries and milk in blender. Cover; process 10 to 15 seconds. To remove seeds, strain mixture through sieve into small bowl; return strained mixture to blender.

2. Add frozen yogurt and vanilla to blender. Cover; process 10 to 15 seconds or until mixture is smooth. Pour into glass. Garnish with raspberries, if desired. Serve immediately.

soy mango smoothie

1   cup frozen mango chunks
1   container (6 ounces) vanilla soy yogurt
½   cup orange juice
2   tablespoons honey
⅛   to ¼ teaspoon grated fresh ginger

1. Place all ingredients in blender. Cover; process 30 to 45 seconds or until mixture is smooth, using on/off pulsing action to break up chunks.

2. Pour into glasses; serve immediately.

frozen apple slushies

½   cup frozen unsweetened apple juice concentrate
1   cup 100% cranberry juice, chilled
1   large (about 10 ounces) Red Delicious apple, peeled and cut into chunks
⅛   teaspoon ground cinnamon
3   cups ice cubes

1. Place apple juice concentrate, cranberry juice, apple chunks and cinnamon in a blender. Cover and blend on HIGH speed until smooth. Add ice cubes, 1 cup at a time, covering and blending on high setting after each addition until smooth and icy. Serve with a straw or spoon.

2. Freeze leftovers in 1-cup servings in small airtight microwave-safe containers. To serve, microwave each serving for 15 seconds then stir. Continue microwaving in 10-second increments until slushy.

orange banana nog

1   cup orange juice
½   cup fat-free milk
½   cup no-cholesterol real egg product
1   small banana, sliced
2   to 3 tablespoons EQUAL® SPOONFUL*
    Ground nutmeg

May substitute 3 to 4½ packets EQUAL® sweetener.

• Blend all ingredients except nutmeg in blender or food processor until smooth; pour into glasses. Sprinkle lightly with nutmeg.

frozen apple slushies

fizzy *fun*

MOUTHWATERING,
FLAVORFUL AND
REFRESHING

ginger-cucumber limeade

MAKES 2¼ CUPS OR 3 (6-OUNCE) SERVINGS

1½ cups chopped, seeded and peeled cucumber
⅓ cup frozen limeade concentrate, thawed
1 teaspoon grated fresh ginger
1 cup club soda or sparkling water, chilled
Ice cubes
Thick cucumber slices (optional)

1. In a blender container combine 1½ cups cucumber, limeade concentrate and ginger. Cover and blend until nearly smooth.

2. In 1-quart pitcher gently stir together cucumber mixture and club soda. Serve immediately over ice cubes. Garnish with cucumber slices, if desired.

ginger-pineapple spritzer

MAKES 3 CUPS OR 4 (6-OUNCE) SERVINGS

2 cups pineapple juice or cranberry juice cocktail

1 tablespoon chopped crystallized ginger

1 cup club soda or sparkling water

Ice cubes

Fresh pineapple wedges (optional)

1. In a small saucepan combine pineapple juice and ginger. Bring to a simmer. Pour into small bowl. Cover and refrigerate for 8 to 24 hours.

2. Strain juice mixture. Discard ginger. Gently stir club soda into juice mixture. Serve in glasses over ice cubes. Garnish with pineapple wedges, if desired.

strawberry-tea fizz

MAKES 2 (8-OUNCE) SERVINGS

1 cup boiling water

4 LIPTON® Green Tea Bags, any variety

2 tablespoons sugar

½ cup seltzer

⅔ cup sliced strawberries and/or raspberries

In teapot, pour boiling water over Lipton Green Tea Bags; cover and brew 1½ minutes. Remove Tea Bags. Stir in sugar and chill.

Just before serving, pour into ice-filled glasses. Add seltzer and strawberries.

ginger-pineapple
spritzer

sparkling tropical fruit combo

MAKES 2¼ CUPS OR 3 (6-OUNCE) SERVINGS

¾ cup orange-tangerine juice or orange juice, chilled

¾ cup passion fruit juice or guava-pineapple juice, chilled

¾ cup club soda or sparkling water, chilled

   Ice cubes

   Maraschino cherries (optional)

1. In a 1-quart pitcher combine orange-tangerine juice and passion fruit juice. Gently stir in club soda.

2. Serve in glasses over ice cubes. Garnish with maraschino cherries, if desired.

tropical spritzer

MAKES 6 (8-OUNCE) SERVINGS

1 cup boiling water

2 LIPTON® "Brisk" Cup Size Tea Bags

½ cup sugar

¼ cup mango fruit juice drink

¼ cup water

3 cups ice cubes (about 18 to 24)

3 cups chilled seltzer

In teapot, pour boiling water over Lipton "Brisk" Cup Size Tea Bags. Cover and brew 5 minutes. Remove Tea Bags; chill.

Meanwhile, in small saucepan, bring sugar, mango fruit juice drink and water to a boil. Reduce heat to low and simmer 5 minutes or until slightly thickened and syrupy. Let cool.

In pitcher, pour mango syrup and tea over ice. Just before serving, stir in seltzer.

sparkling tropical
fruit combo

cool strawberry drink

MAKES 4 SERVINGS

1   fresh pineapple
1   cup fresh strawberries, hulled and halved
2   teaspoons sugar
1   pint lemon sherbet
4   cups chilled lemon-lime beverage or ginger ale

1. To prepare pineapple, cut off both ends. Remove rind and eyes with sharp knife. Cut pineapple into lengthwise quarters. Remove core; cut fruit into chunks. Measure 1 cup pineapple; refrigerate remaining pineapple for another use.

2. Place 1 cup pineapple and strawberries in a large bowl. Sprinkle with sugar. Let stand until ready to use.

3. Divide fruit among 4 large glasses. Add ½ cup sherbet to each glass. Pour 1 cup lemon-lime beverage into each glass. Serve immediately.

fruity spritzer

MAKES 1 SERVING

1   teaspoon strawberry extract
2   sugar cubes
1   cup chilled seltzer water

Place strawberry extract in small bowl; add sugar cubes and let stand 5 minutes. Place flavored sugar cubes in bottom of glass and add seltzer. Let cubes dissolve; serve immediately.

Favorite recipe from **The Sugar Association, Inc.**

nectarine mocktails

3   fresh California nectarines, halved, pitted and diced

1   container (10 ounces) unsweetened frozen strawberries, partially thawed

1   bottle (28 ounces) club soda or sugar-free ginger ale

8   mint sprigs (optional)

Add nectarines, strawberries and 1 cup club soda to blender. Process until smooth. Pour into chilled glasses about ⅔ full. Top with remaining club soda. Garnish with mint, if desired.

Favorite recipe from **California Tree Fruit Agreement**

white sangria

MAKES 8 TO 10 (10-OUNCE) SERVINGS

- 2   oranges, cut into ¼-inch slices
- 2   lemons, cut into ¼-inch slices
- ½   cup sugar
- 2   bottles dry, fruity white wine (such as Pinot Grigio), chilled
- ½   cup peach schnapps
- 3   ripe peaches, pit removed and cut into wedges
- 2   cups ice cubes (about 16 cubes)

1. Place orange and lemon slices in large punch bowl. Pour sugar over orange and lemon slices. Using a wooden spoon, lightly mash together until sugar dissolves and fruit begins to break down.

2. Stir in wine, peach schnapps and peach wedges. Refrigerate at least 2 hours or up to 10. Add ice cubes just before serving.

sweet 'n sour grape fizz

MAKES 1 SERVING

- 3   ounces MR & MRS T® Sweet & Sour Mix
- 3   ounces white grape juice
- 1½   ounces rum
- ½   ounce ROSE'S® Lime Juice
- 1   ounce club soda
- ½   cup ice
       Frozen grapes*

For frozen grapes, simply rinse grapes under cold running water and place in the freezer until frozen (15 to 20 minutes).

Pour first 5 ingredients into shaker with ice. Strain contents into glass and garnish with frozen grapes.

white sangria

pineapple agua fresca

3 cups fresh pineapple chunks, 1-inch pieces (1 small or ½ of 1 large pineapple)

¼ cup fresh lime juice

2 tablespoons minced fresh mint

⅓ cup sugar

2 cups club soda, well chilled

Ice

6 mint sprigs

1. Place pineapple, lime juice, mint and sugar in blender container. Blend on HIGH until mixture is frothy, about 30 seconds to 1 minute.

2. Pour into a tall pitcher. Add club soda and stir once or twice to mix. Immediately pour into 6 sugar-dipped (*see page* 4), ice-filled glasses. Garnish each serving with a mint sprig.

easy orange fizz

MAKES 4 (6-OUNCE) SERVINGS

Maraschino cherries

Mint leaves

1 (6-ounce) can frozen Florida orange juice concentrate, thawed

Club soda or tonic water, chilled

Thoroughly drain maraschino cherries. Arrange mint leaves and cherries in compartments of ice cube trays; fill with water and freeze until firm to form decorative ice cubes.

Prepare orange juice concentrate according to label directions, except substitute club soda or tonic water for the water. Pour into glasses over decorative ice cubes. Serve at once.

Favorite recipe from **Florida Department of Citrus**

pineapple agua fresca

lemon and pomegranate refresher

3	bags hibiscus, lemon tea
1½	cups boiling water
⅓	cup sugar
3	tablespoons fresh lemon juice
1½	cups pomegranate juice
1	cup club soda, well chilled
	Ice
4	lemon wedges

1. Place tea bags in a large heatproof mug or pitcher. Add boiling water. Steep tea for 5 minutes. Remove and discard tea bags. Refrigerate until cold.

2. Combine tea, sugar, lemon juice and pomegranate juice in a tall pitcher. Stir well. (This can be done in advance and kept chilled for several hours.) Just before serving pour in the club soda and stir once or twice to mix.

3. Pour into 4 sugar-dipped (*see page* 4), ice-filled glasses. Garnish with a lemon wedge.

grapefruit sparkler

2	tablespoons frozen pink grapefruit juice concentrate
¾	cup white cranberry juice
	Ice cubes
	Seltzer water

1. In tall glass stir grapefruit juice concentrate and cranberry juice together until concentrate is dissolved.

2. Add 3 ice cubes and top off with seltzer water. Stir to combine.

lemon and
pomegranate refresher

cranberry lime ricky

- ½ cup cranberry juice
- 2 tablespoons grenadine
- 2 tablespoons lime juice
- ½ cup seltzer water

1. Place 6 ice cubes in tall glass.

2. Pour cranberry juice, grenadine and lime juice over ice cubes. Stir until well combined and cool. Pour in seltzer water and serve.

chili-spiked fresh lemonade spritzer

- 3 cups water
- 1¼ cups sugar
- 5 to 10 small dried hot red chilies*
- 2 cups fresh lemon juice
- 1 bottle (750 ml) Asti Spumante or club soda
  Additional sugar (optional)
  Ice
  Lime wedges and dried hot red chilies for garnish

Use chilies according to taste.

1. Combine water, 1¼ cups sugar and chilies in medium saucepan. Cook and stir over high heat until mixture comes to a boil and sugar dissolves. Reduce heat to low; cover and simmer 30 minutes. Remove from heat and cool completely. Refrigerate 2 hours or up to 3 days.

2. Pour mixture through strainer into 3-quart pitcher; discard chilies. Stir in lemon juice and Asti Spumante. Stir in additional sugar to taste. Serve over ice. Garnish, if desired.

cranberry lime ricky

sparkling strawberry-lime shakes

2 cups (10 ounces) frozen whole unsweetened strawberries

1¼ cups lime-flavored sparkling water, divided

¼ cup whipping cream or half-and-half

1 tablespoon sugar substitute

Lime wedges or slices

1. Place strawberries in blender; allow to thaw 5 minutes before proceeding. Add 1 cup sparkling water, cream and sugar substitute. Cover; blend until smooth, scraping down side of blender once or twice (mixture will be thick).

2. Gently stir in remaining sparkling water; pour into 2 glasses. Garnish with lime wedges.

Variations: For a tropical variation, add 1 teaspoon banana extract and/or ½ teaspoon coconut extract along with the cream. For a rum-flavored drink add ½ teaspoon rum extract.

Tip: For quick shakes anytime, wash, hull and freeze whole strawberries in a tightly covered container.

sparkling ginger-apple cider

MAKES 1 (12-OUNCE) SERVING

¾ cup apple juice

¾ cup ginger ale

⅛ teaspoon vanilla

Place 3 ice cubes in tall glass. Pour apple juice, ginger ale and vanilla on top; stir until combined.

Variation: Sparkling Apple-Ginger Float: Prepare as directed, omitting ice cubes. Float scoop of vanilla ice cream on top.

sparkling strawberry-lime shakes

chocolate heaven

INDULGE YOURSELF
DAY OR NIGHT

mocha cooler

MAKES 1 SERVING

1 cup milk

1 tablespoon instant coffee granules

1 tablespoon chocolate syrup

¼ cup vanilla or coffee ice cream

Whipped Topping (optional)

Chocolate Shavings (optional)

Chocolate-covered coffee beans (optional)

Combine milk, coffee, syrup and ice cream in blender. Purée until smooth. Garnish with whipped topping, chocolate shavings and coffee beans if desired.

mysterious chocolate mint cooler

MAKES ABOUT 2 (10-OUNCE) SERVINGS

- 2 cups cold milk or half-and-half
- ¼ cup chocolate syrup
- 1 teaspoon peppermint extract
- Crushed ice
- Aerosol whipped topping
- Mint leaves

Combine milk, chocolate syrup and peppermint extract in small pitcher; stir until well blended. Fill 2 glasses with crushed ice. Pour chocolate-mint mixture over ice. Top with whipped topping. Garnish with mint leaves.

slimming chocoberry splash

MAKES 2 (6-OUNCE) SERVINGS

- Crushed ice
- ¾ cup cold nonfat milk
- ¼ cup sliced fresh strawberries
- 2 tablespoons HERSHEY®S Syrup
- 2 tablespoons vanilla ice milk
- 2 tablespoons club soda

1. Fill two tall glasses with crushed ice.

2. Place all remaining ingredients except club soda in blender container. Cover; blend until smooth. Pour into glasses over crushed ice; add club soda. Serve immediately. Garnish as desired.

Variation: Substitute any of the following for strawberries: ⅓ cup drained canned peach slices, 3 tablespoons frozen raspberries, 2 pineapple slices or ¼ cup drained crushed canned pineapple.

mysterious chocolate mint cooler

chocolate new york egg cream

1   square (1 ounce) semisweet chocolate (optional)

¼   cup chocolate syrup

1   cup chilled club soda or carbonated mineral water

    Ice

1. Shave chocolate with vegetable peeler, if desired. (Makes about ½ cup.)

2. Pour syrup into 12-ounce glass. Stir in club soda until foamy. Add ice. Garnish with 1 teaspoon chocolate shavings.* Serve immediately.

*Cover and refrigerate leftover chocolate shavings for another use.

mocha shake

¼   cup warm water

2   tablespoons HERSHEY®S Cocoa

1   tablespoon sugar

1   to 2 teaspoons powdered instant coffee

½   cup milk

2   cups vanilla ice cream

Place water, cocoa, sugar and instant coffee in blender container. Cover; blend briefly on low speed. Add milk. Cover; blend well on high speed. Add ice cream. Cover; blend until smooth. Serve immediately. Garnish as desired.

Know Your Cocoa: Unsweetened cocoa is formed by extracting most of the cocoa butter from pure chocolate and grinding the remaining chocolate solids into a powder. "Dutch process" cocoa is unsweetened cocoa that has been treated with an alkali, giving it a darker appearance and a slightly less bitter flavor.

chocolate new york egg cream

peachy chocolate yogurt shake

MAKES 4 SERVINGS

⅔ cup peeled fresh peach slices or 1 package (10 ounces) frozen peach slices, thawed and drained

¼ teaspoon almond extract

2 cups (1 pint) vanilla nonfat frozen yogurt

¼ cup HERSHEY'S Syrup

¼ cup nonfat milk

Place peaches and almond extract in blender container. Cover; blend until smooth. Add frozen yogurt, syrup and milk. Cover; blend until smooth. Serve immediately.

peanut butter chocolate twist shake

MAKES 1 SERVING

6 ounces frozen vanilla yogurt or ice cream

4 ounces coconut juice or milk

1 ounce chocolate chips

1 ounce peanut butter

2 curls shaved chocolate

½ ounce crushed roasted peanuts

Whip all ingredients except shaved chocolate and peanuts together in blender until smooth. Garnish with shaved chocolate and crushed roasted peanuts.

Favorite recipe from **Peanut Advisory Board**

peachy chocolate yogurt shake

healthful delights

TASTY, FULFILLING AND GOOD FOR YOU, TOO

cantaloupe smoothie

MAKES 3½ CUPS OR ABOUT 4 (6-OUNCE) SERVINGS

3   cups seeded, peeled and cubed cantaloupe
2   containers (6 ounces each) orange crème low-fat yogurt
½   cup orange-tangerine juice or orange juice, chilled
1   tablespoon honey
1   teaspoon vanilla
4   small cantaloupe wedges (optional)

1. In blender container combine cubed cantaloupe, yogurt, juice, honey and vanilla. Cover and blend until nearly smooth.

2. Pour into glasses. Garnish with cantaloupe wedges, if desired. Serve immediately.

chocolate-blueberry soy shake

MAKES 1 SERVING

5 ounces (½ cup plus 2 tablespoons) soymilk

2 tablespoons frozen or fresh blueberries (about 20 berries)

¼ teaspoon unsweetened cocoa powder

¼ cup crushed ice

Place all ingredients in blender; blend at high speed 30 seconds or until well blended. Pour into chilled glass to serve.

fruit 'n juice breakfast shake

MAKES 2 SERVINGS

1 extra-ripe medium DOLE® Banana

¾ cup DOLE® Pineapple Juice

½ cup lowfat vanilla yogurt

½ cup DOLE® Fresh Frozen Blueberries

Combine all ingredients in blender. Process until smooth.

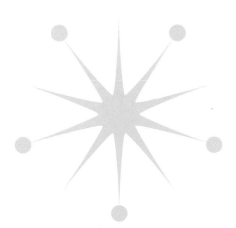

chocolate-blueberry
soy shake

spiced passion fruit-yogurt starter

MAKES 2⅓ CUPS OR ABOUT 3 (6-OUNCE) SERVINGS

- 1 cup plain fat-free yogurt
- 1 medium ripe banana, cut into pieces
- 1 cup sliced fresh strawberries
- ¼ cup frozen passion fruit juice concentrate or frozen apple-passion-mango fruit juice concentrate, thawed
- ¾ teaspoon pumpkin pie spice
- ⅛ teaspoon ground white pepper

1. In blender container combine yogurt, banana, strawberries, passion fruit juice concentrate, pumpkin pie spice and white pepper. Cover and process until nearly smooth.

2. Pour into glasses. Serve immediately.

soy milk smoothie

MAKES 4 SERVINGS

- 3 cups plain or vanilla soy milk
- 1 banana, peeled and frozen (see Tip)
- 1 cup frozen strawberries or raspberries
- 1 teaspoon vanilla or almond extract
- ⅓ cup EQUAL® SPOONFUL*

May substitute 8 packets EQUAL® sweetener.

• Place all ingredients in blender or food processor. Blend until smooth.

Tip: Peel and cut banana into large chunks. Place in plastic freezer bag, seal and freeze at least 5 to 6 hours or overnight.

spiced passion
fruit-yogurt
starter

morning glory cream fizz

MAKES 2¼ CUPS OR 3 (6-OUNCE) SERVINGS

1   ripe banana, cut into chunks

1   cup peeled, seeded and cubed papaya or mango

3   tablespoons fat-free half-and-half or milk

1   container (6 ounces) vanilla low-fat yogurt

1   tablespoon honey

½   cup club soda or sparkling water, chilled

    Ground nutmeg

1. In blender container combine banana, papaya, half-and-half, yogurt and honey. Cover and process until nearly smooth.

2. Gently stir club soda into fruit mixture. Pour into glasses. Sprinkle with nutmeg. Serve immediately.

orange-pineapple breakfast shake with yogurt & honey

MAKES 2 SERVINGS

1   cup Florida orange or tangerine juice

½   cup unsweetened pineapple juice

½   cup plain low fat yogurt

1   teaspoon honey

    Orange twists or fresh mint leaves for garnish (optional)

Add orange juice, pineapple juice, yogurt and honey to food processor or blender. Process until smooth. Pour into two glasses. Garnish with orange twists or fresh mint sprigs, if desired. Serve immediately.

Favorite recipe from **Florida Department of Citrus**

morning glory cream fizz

anti-stress smoothie

1 cup vanilla low-fat frozen yogurt

1 medium-size ripe banana

2 cups frozen blueberries

1 tablespoon honey

1 cup reduced-fat (2%) milk

4 to 6 ice cubes

1. Place yogurt, banana, blueberries, honey and milk in blender container. Blend on HIGH until mixture is frothy and ice cubes are finely ground, about 30 seconds to 1 minute.

2. Pour into 4 glasses.

Note: Lavender is a calming agent. If your supermarket or floral shop has unsprayed sprigs of lavender, remove the flowering buds and sprinkle about ½ teaspoon over each serving. Or, garnish each smoothie with a sprig of lavender.

pear yogurt shake

MAKES 4 CUPS

1 can (16 ounces) pears in juice, chilled

1 cup low-fat plain yogurt

1 banana, peeled

3 ice cubes, crushed

2 tablespoons honey

Dash ground nutmeg

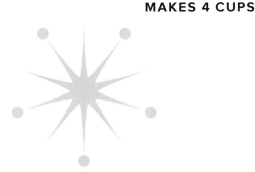

Combine pears with juice, yogurt, banana, ice and honey in blender or food processor; blend until smooth. Pour shake into chilled glasses. Sprinkle with nutmeg and serve immediately.

Favorite recipe from **National Honey Board**

anti-stress smoothie

protein energy shake

- 1 cup plain soy milk
- 1½ cups vanilla soy yogurt
- ¼ cup raw walnut halves
- ¼ teaspoon ground cinnamon
- 2½ tablespoons honey
- 4 ice cubes

1. Combine soy milk, soy yogurt, walnuts, cinnamon, honey and ice cubes in blender container.

2. Blend on HIGH until mixture is frothy and ice cubes are finely ground, about 30 seconds to 1 minute. Pour into 4 glasses.

mango yogurt drink

- ½ cup plain yogurt
- 1 ripe mango, peeled, seeded and sliced
- ¼ cup orange juice
- 1 teaspoon honey
- 2 ice cubes
- Milk (optional)

Place all ingredients in blender. Cover; process until smooth. Add milk to obtain preferred consistency.

Tip: The skin of most mangoes tinges with more red or yellow as the fruit ripens. Mangoes are ready to eat when they yield to gentle pressure.

protein energy shake

berry soy-cream blend

MAKES 2 SERVINGS

2   cups frozen mixed berries
1   can (14 ounces) blackberries, with juice
1   cup almond milk or soy milk
1   cup apple juice
½   cup (4 ounces) soft tofu enriched with calcium

Place all ingredients in blender. Cover; blend on HIGH speed until smooth. Divide between 2 glasses; serve immediately.

Tip: If your child is allergic to dairy products, make this thick berry shake for creamy texture and sweet fruity flavors. Tofu is also high in protein, good for growing children.

banana-pineapple breakfast shake

MAKES 4 SERVINGS

2   cups plain fat-free yogurt
1   can (8 ounces) crushed pineapple in juice, undrained
1   ripe medium banana
8   packets sugar substitute
1   teaspoon vanilla
⅛   teaspoon ground nutmeg
1   cup ice cubes
    Fresh pineapple slices (optional)

Place all ingredients in blender. Cover; blend until smooth. Pour into 4 serving glasses. Garnish with pineapple slices.

Tip: This recipe is perfect for a party or another special occasion. Double the ingredient amounts, and you'll have enough for everyone to enjoy!

berry soy-cream blend

tofu orange dream

½   cup soft tofu

½   cup orange juice

1   container (about 2½ ounces) baby food carrots

2   tablespoons honey or 1 tablespoon sugar

¼   teaspoon grated fresh ginger

2   to 3 ice cubes

Place all ingredients in blender. Cover; process 15 seconds until smooth. Pour into glass; serve immediately.

coffee&tea

JAZZ UP A CLASSIC
BEVERAGE

chipotle chili-spiked mocha slush

MAKES 1½ CUPS OR 2 (6-OUNCE) SERVINGS

1	package (1.0 to 1.25 ounces) instant hot chocolate mix without marshmallows
½	teaspoon instant coffee crystals
⅛	teaspoon chipotle chili powder
⅛	teaspoon ground cinnamon
¾	cup hot water
1	cup coffee, vanilla or chocolate ice cream
⅓	cup fat-free half-and-half
	Whipped cream (optional)
	Ground cinnamon (optional)

1. In 2-cup glass measure stir together hot chocolate mix, coffee crystals, chili powder and ground cinnamon. Stir in hot water until combined. Pour into ice cube tray. Freeze until firm.

2. In blender container combine chocolate ice cubes, ice cream and half-and-half. Cover and blend until smooth. Pour into glasses. Serve immediately topped with whipped cream and cinnamon, if desired.

almond milk tea with tapioca

3½	cups water
2	black tea bags
4	teaspoons sugar
¼	teaspoon almond extract, divided
1	tablespoon instant tapioca
¼	cup whole milk, divided

1. Bring water to a boil in medium saucepan over medium-high heat.

2. Pour 2 cups of boiling water over tea bags in teapot or 2-cup heatproof measuring cup. Steep tea 4 minutes or until very dark. Remove tea bags from teapot; discard. Stir in sugar and almond extract and set aside to cool.

3. Meanwhile, add tapioca to remaining 1½ cups boiling water and continue to boil over medium-high heat until tapioca is translucent and cooked through, 3 to 4 minutes. Transfer tapioca to fine-mesh strainer and rinse under cold water until cool to the touch.

4. Divide tapioca between 2 tall glasses, then pour 2 tablespoons milk into each glass. Fill each glass three-fourths full with ice. Divide tea between glasses; stir to combine and serve immediately.

Variations: Substitute your favorite herbal or fruit flavored tea for the black tea. This recipe is also excellent when vanilla is substituted for almond extract.

green tea citrus smoothie

4   green tea bags

1   cup boiling water

3   tablespoons sugar

3   tablespoons lemon juice

1   cup frozen lemon sorbet

4   ice cubes, plus extra for glasses

1   cup club soda, well chilled

4   lemon wedges

1. Place tea bags in heatproof cup or mug. Add boiling water. Steep tea 5 minutes. Remove and discard tea bags. Refrigerate until cold.

2. Place tea, sugar, lemon juice, lemon sorbet and 4 ice cubes in blender container. Blend on HIGH until mixture is frothy and ice cubes are finely ground, about 30 seconds to 1 minute.

3. Pour into a pitcher. Add club soda and stir briefly to mix. Pour into 4 ice-filled glasses and garnish with a lemon wedge.

frosty raspberry lemon tea

MAKES 2 SERVINGS

1   cup brewed lemon-flavored herbal tea, at room temperature

1   cup water

½   cup frozen unsweetened raspberries

1½   cups ice

Combine all ingredients in large blender container. Blend on high speed until smooth, pulsing as necessary to break up all ice. Pour into 2 tall glasses and serve immediately.

green tea citrus smoothie

green tea lychee frappé

1   can (15 ounces) lychees in syrup,* undrained

2   cups water

2   slices peeled ginger (¼ inch thick, 2 inches wide)

3   green tea bags

Canned lychees are readily available in either the canned fruit or ethnic foods section of most large supermarkets.

1. Drain syrup from lychees, reserving syrup. Place lychees in single layer in medium resealable food storage bag; place in freezer until frozen. Cover and refrigerate syrup.

2. Heat water and ginger in small saucepan over medium-high heat until water begins to steam and barely simmer. Remove from heat; add tea bags. Let steep 3 minutes. Discard ginger and tea bags. Pour tea into heat-resistant pitcher; cover and refrigerate until cool.

3. Place frozen lychees, chilled green tea, and ½ cup reserved syrup in blender. Blend on HIGH until smooth and well combined, about 20 seconds. Serve immediately.

Note: A lychee is a subtropical fruit grown in China, Mexico and the United States. It is a small oval fruit with a rough, bright red hull. Beneath the hull is milky white flesh surrounding a single seed. The flesh is sweet and juicy. The fresh lychee is a delicacy in China. They are available fresh at Asian markets in the United States in early summer. Canned lychees are readily available. They are most often served as dessert.

ginger and apple spritzer

3 English breakfast tea bags

1 cup boiling water

2 tablespoons minced crystallized ginger, plus additional for garnish

¼ cup sugar

2 tablespoons lemon juice

3 cups sparkling apple cider, well chilled

Ice

4 to 6 lemon wedges

1. Place tea bags in heatproof cup or mug. Add boiling water. Steep tea for 5 minutes. Remove and discard tea bags. Refrigerate until cold.

2. Combine tea, ginger, sugar and lemon juice in a tall pitcher. Stir well. (This can be done in advance and kept chilled for several hours.) Just before serving pour in the sparkling apple cider and stir once or twice to mix.

3. Pour into 4 to 6 ice-filled glasses. Spoon a little of the minced ginger into each glass. Garnish with a lemon wedge.

mango-mint green tea

3   cups boiling water

6   green tea bags

¼   cup fresh mint leaves

1½ cups mango-peach juice or mango nectar

2   tablespoons sugar

    Ice cubes

    Fresh mango slices (optional)

1. In medium bowl pour water over tea bags. Let steep for 5 minutes. Remove and discard tea bags.

2. Meanwhile, use back of spoon to slightly crush mint leaves.

3. Stir mint leaves, mango-peach juice and sugar into tea. Cover and refrigerate for 4 to 24 hours.

4. Stir tea. Strain out mint leaves; discard. Serve tea over ice cubes. Garnish with fresh mango slices, if desired.

minty green tea lemonade

4   cups boiling water

6   LIPTON® Green Tea Bags

2½ cups cold water

1   can (12 ounces) frozen lemonade concentrate

½   cup loosely packed fresh mint leaves

In teapot, pour boiling water over Lipton Green Tea Bags; cover and brew 2 minutes. Remove tea bags and let cool.

In 2-quart pitcher, combine all ingredients; chill at least 2 hours. Strain, if desired. Serve in ice-filled glasses. Garnish, if desired, with lemon wedges.

rosemary-mint sun tea

MAKES 6 CUPS OR 8 (6-OUNCE) SERVINGS

6   tea bags

6   cups cold water

3   (3- to 4-inch-long) sprigs fresh rosemary

1   (3- to 4-inch-long) sprig fresh mint
    Ice cubes
    Lemon slices (optional)
    Fresh rosemary (optional)

1. In 2-quart clear glass container combine tea bags and water.

2. Use back of spoon to slightly crush fresh rosemary and fresh mint sprigs. Add to water and tea bags in glass container. Let stand at room temperature for 4 hours.

3. Strain out tea bags and fresh herb sprigs; discard. Cover and chill tea. Serve over ice cubes with lemon slices, if desired. Garnish with fresh rosemary, if desired.

iced mocha

MAKES 2 SERVINGS

2   cups strongly brewed coffee

¾   cup skim milk

1   tablespoon packed brown sugar

½   teaspoon unsweetened cocoa powder
     Ice

Add coffee, milk, sugar and cocoa to blender. Process until smooth. Pour over ice and serve immediately, or refrigerate, stir well and serve over ice.

Favorite recipe from **The Sugar Association, Inc.**

tropical arnold palmer

48   mint leaves (from 2 or 3 bunches of mint)

4   cups water, plus about 3 cups additional for filling ice trays

5   tropical fruit-flavor green tea bags (such as passion fruit, peach or mango)

¾   cup frozen raspberry lemonade concentrate

1   lemon, cut into thin wedges, for garnish

1. Place 2 mint leaves in each of compartment of 2 ice cube trays (24 compartments total). Fill with water and place in freezer until frozen.

2. Heat remaining 4 cups water in medium saucepan over medium-high heat until water begins to steam and barely simmer, about 4 minutes. Remove from heat, add tea bags, and steep 3 minutes. Discard tea bags. Add frozen lemonade concentrate and stir until dissolved. Set aside to cool slightly.

3. Place 12 mint ice cubes in serving pitcher. Pour tea mixture over ice and stir until ice cubes dissolve.

4. Divide remaining 12 ice cubes among 4 glasses and fill each glass with beverage. Garnish with lemon wedges.

iced mexican coffee

½   cup regular or decaffeinated ground dark roast coffee

4   cups water*

1   tablespoon sugar

⅔   cup fat-free half-and-half or milk

¼   cup chocolate syrup

1   teaspoon vanilla

½   teaspoon cinnamon extract**

Ice cubes

1. Place ground coffee in filter basket of coffee maker. Add water to coffee maker and brew according to manufacturer's directions. Discard coffee grounds. Pour coffee into small pitcher. Stir sugar into coffee until dissolved. Cover and cool about 2 hours or until coffee reaches room temperature.

2. In small bowl stir together half-and-half, chocolate syrup, vanilla and cinnamon extract. Stir into cooled coffee. Pour over ice cubes. Serve immediately.

Use measuring cup (not coffee maker measures) to measure water.

**If desired, omit cinnamon extract and break 2 (3-inch-long) pieces of stick cinnamon into several pieces. Place cinnamon pieces into filter basket of coffee maker, along with ground coffee. Continue as directed above.*

party punches

CELEBRATE IN STYLE WITH A DELICIOUS, FESTIVE DRINK

cranberry-pineapple punch

· ·

MAKES 7 CUPS OR ABOUT 9 (6-OUNCE) SERVINGS

2½ cups cranberry juice cocktail, chilled
2 cups pineapple juice, chilled
½ teaspoon almond extract
2½ cups carbonated ginger ale beverage, chilled
Ice cubes

1. In large pitcher combine cranberry juice, pineapple juice and almond extract. Gently stir in ginger ale.

2. Serve over ice cubes.

cuban guava punch

2   cups water

¾   cup sugar

1½   cups guava nectar or ruby red grapefruit juice drink*, chilled

1½   cups orange juice, chilled

½   cup pineapple juice, chilled

¼   cup lime juice*

Ice cubes

Fresh pineapple wedges (optional)

1. In small saucepan combine water and sugar. Cook and stir over medium heat until sugar dissolves. Let stand at least 2 hours or until room temperature.

2. In 2-quart pitcher combine sugar mixture, guava nectar, orange juice, pineapple juice and lime juice; mix well. Serve over ice cubes. Garnish with fresh pineapple wedge, if desired.

*If using ruby red grapefruit juice drink, reduce lime juice to 2 tablespoons.

strawberry-mango daiquiri punch

MAKES 7 CUPS OR ABOUT 9 (6-OUNCE) SERVINGS

3	cups cut-up, peeled and seeded fresh mango
¾	cup frozen limeade concentrate, thawed
3	cups frozen unsweetened whole strawberries
¾	cup light rum or pineapple juice
2½	cups lemon-lime carbonated beverage
	Ice cubes
	Fresh strawberries (optional)

1. In blender container combine half of the mango pieces and limeade concentrate. Cover and blend until nearly smooth. Add half the strawberries, a few berries at a time, through the hole in the blender lid. Blend until nearly smooth. Pour into 2½-quart pitcher.

2. In same blender container combine remaining mango pieces and rum. Cover and blend until nearly smooth. Add remaining strawberries, a few berries at a time, through the hole in the blender lid. Blend until nearly smooth. Add to mango mixture in pitcher. Mix well.

3. Gently stir in carbonated beverage. Serve over ice cubes. Garnish with fresh strawberries, if desired.

pineapple-lemonade pizzazz

MAKES 12 CUPS OR 16 (6-OUNCE) SERVINGS

3   cups peach nectar, mango nectar, peach-mango juice or passion fruit juice, chilled

3   cups pineapple juice, chilled

1   can (12 ounces) frozen lemonade concentrate, thawed

1   bottle (16.9 ounces) carbonated ginger ale beverage, chilled

2½ cups club soda or sparkling water, chilled

    Crushed ice

1. In a 1-gallon pitcher combine peach nectar, pineapple juice and lemonade concentrate.

2. Gently stir in carbonated ginger ale and club soda. Immediately serve over crushed ice.

pineapple raspberry punch

MAKES 9 CUPS

5   cups DOLE® Pineapple Juice

1   quart raspberry cranberry drink

1   pint fresh or frozen raspberries

1   lemon, thinly sliced

    Ice

• Chill ingredients. Combine in punch bowl.

pineapple-lemonade pizzazz

festive citrus punch

MAKES ABOUT 18 (4-OUNCE) SERVINGS

1   can (6 ounces) frozen Florida grapefruit juice concentrate, thawed
1   can (6 ounces) frozen pineapple juice concentrate, thawed
1   cup water
3   tablespoons honey
2   tablespoons grenadine syrup (optional)
1   bottle (1 liter) ginger ale, chilled
    Mint sprigs for garnish (optional)
    Ice cubes

1. Combine grapefruit juice, pineapple juice, water and honey in punch bowl or large pitcher. Stir in grenadine, if desired. Stir until well combined.

2. Just before serving, slowly pour ginger ale down side of punch bowl. Stir gently to combine. Garnish, if desired. Serve over ice in chilled glasses.

Favorite recipe from **Florida Department of Citrus**

pomegranate green tea punch

MAKES 4 (8-OUNCE) SERVINGS

3   cups boiling water
6   LIPTON® Green Tea Bags
2   tablespoons sugar
1   cup chilled pomegranate juice or cranberry juice cocktail

In teapot, pour boiling water over Lipton Green Tea Bags; cover and brew 1½ minutes. Remove Tea Bags; stir in sugar and cool.

In large pitcher, combine tea and pomegranate juice. Chill, if desired, or serve in ice-filled glasses. Enjoy!

festive citrus punch

orange iced tea

2   SUNKIST® oranges

4   cups boiling water

5   tea bags

   Ice cubes

   Honey or brown sugar to taste

With vegetable peeler, peel each orange in continuous spiral, removing only outer colored layer of peel (eat peeled fruit or save for other uses). In large pitcher, pour boiling water over tea bags and orange peel. Cover and steep 5 minutes. Remove tea bags; chill tea mixture with peel in covered container. To serve, remove peel and pour over ice cubes in tall glasses. Sweeten to taste with honey. Garnish with orange quarter-cartwheel slices and fresh mint leaves, if desired.

strawberry-apricot punch

MAKES 12 SERVINGS

2   packages (10 ounces each) frozen sliced strawberries in syrup, thawed

2   cans (5½ ounces each) apricot or peach nectar

¼   cup lemon juice

2   tablespoons honey

1   bottle (2 liters) lemon-lime soda

   Lemon slices or fresh strawberry halves (optional)

1. Place strawberries with syrup in food processor; process until smooth.

2. Pour puréed strawberries into large punch bowl. Stir in apricot nectar, lemon juice and honey; blend well.

3. To serve, stir soda into strawberry mixture. Garnish, if desired.

orange iced tea

piña colada punch

MAKES 12 (½ CUP) SERVINGS

- 3 cups water
- 10 whole cloves
- 4 cardamom pods
- 2 sticks cinnamon
- 1 pint piña colada low-fat frozen yogurt, softened*
- 1 can (12 ounces) frozen pineapple juice concentrate, thawed
- 1¼ cups lemon seltzer water
- 1¼ teaspoons rum extract
- ¾ teaspoon coconut extract (optional)
  Mint sprigs (optional)

***Can substitute pineapple sherbet for piña colada low-fat frozen yogurt. When using
pineapple sherbet, use coconut extract for more authentic flavor.**

1. Combine water, cloves, cardamom and cinnamon in small saucepan. Bring to a
boil over high heat; reduce heat to low. Simmer, covered, 5 minutes; cool. Strain
spices; discard.

2. Combine spiced water, frozen yogurt and juice concentrate in small punch bowl
or pitcher. Stir until frozen yogurt is melted. Stir in seltzer water, rum extract and
coconut extract, if desired. Garnish with mint sprigs.

strawberry champagne punch

2   packages (10 ounces each) frozen sliced strawberries in syrup, thawed

2   cans (5½ ounces each) apricot or peach nectar

¼   cup lemon juice

2   tablespoons honey

2   bottles (750 mL each) champagne or sparkling white wine, chilled

    Lemon slices, fresh strawberry halves and mint leaves for garnish (optional)

1. Place strawberries with syrup in food processor; process until smooth.

2. Pour puréed strawberries into large punch bowl. Stir in apricot nectar, lemon juice and honey; blend well. Refrigerate until serving time.

3. To serve, stir champagne into strawberry mixture. Garnish, if desired.

Cutting Corners: To save time, thaw the strawberries in the refrigerator the day before using them.

index

acknowledgments

The publisher would like to thank the companies and organizations listed below for the use of their recipes and photographs in this publication.

California Tree Fruit Agreement
Dole Food Company, Inc.
Equal® sweetener
Florida Department of Citrus
The Hershey Company
Mr & Mrs T® is a registered
trademark of Mott's, LLP
National Honey Board

Peanut Advisory Board
The Sugar Association, Inc.
Reprinted with permission of
Sunkist Growers, Inc.
All Rights Reserved.
Unilever
U.S. Highbush Blueberry Council